ELIZABETH COLE

MY WAY TO
MAKING FRIENDS

ILLUSTRATED BY
TATYANA KIM

Good friends are like stars.
You don't always see them, but you know they're
always there.

Book by Elizabeth Cole

This book belongs to

....

....

Melissa was a little girl, who was quiet and shy.
She was often lonely and didn't know why.
When she tried to make friends, she didn't succeed.
For Melissa, making friends was very hard indeed.

One day, she saw children playing in a sand-pit.
She wanted to join them, but chose to avoid it.
Melissa felt shy, timid and insecure too.
She didn't know what to say or what to do.

Just as she was about to go away,
a girl invited little Melissa to play.
She said, "Come and build with me!
Our sandcastle will win! You'll see!"

Melissa joined the girl and had lots of fun;
but the rival team was better, and they won.
Melissa was upset, she couldn't stand it.
So she ruined the castle and left the sand pit.

Melissa ran home and hugged her teddy.
To fall asleep, the little girl was ready.
"Teddy, you are the only friend I need,"
Melissa said, and meant it indeed.

The dream took them to a tropical place.
Melissa felt the hot sun on her face.
"Welcome to the Jungle of Friendship!" she heard.
The girl saw not just one giraffe, but a whole herd!

"You will make a lot of friends here.
Come and meet the others, my dear,"
the giraffe said, but Melissa replied, "No!"
How to make friends? I simply don't know!"

"Start the conversation by asking a name.
Simply saying 'hello' can lead to a game.
'You have a nice toy' is also a good way.
You might offer snacks or invite them to play."

"Those are some of the ways that I use.
There are many others from which to choose.
You might try a different way for each friend.
Choose the one that suits you best in the end!"

Later, they saw two zebras at play.
Melissa decided to try the "Hello" way.
She introduced herself, offering her name,
and both of the zebras did the same.

"We love hopscotch. What about you?
You can join us and bring your teddy too,"
the zebra said, and they began to play.
Melissa thought, what a good way!

Melissa lost the game, but what a surprise!
The little girl could hardly believe her eyes.
One of the zebras, who lost the game too,
said to the winner, "I'm so happy for you!"

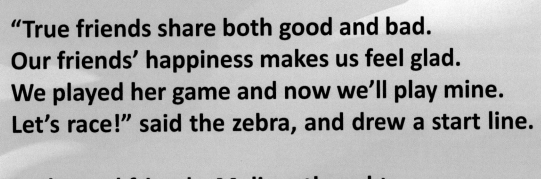

"True friends share both good and bad.
Our friends' happiness makes us feel glad.
We played her game and now we'll play mine.
Let's race!" said the zebra, and drew a start line.

Such good friends, Melissa thought.
The little girl admired the zebras a lot.

Then she met a monkey in the park.
He was sad because he got a bad mark.

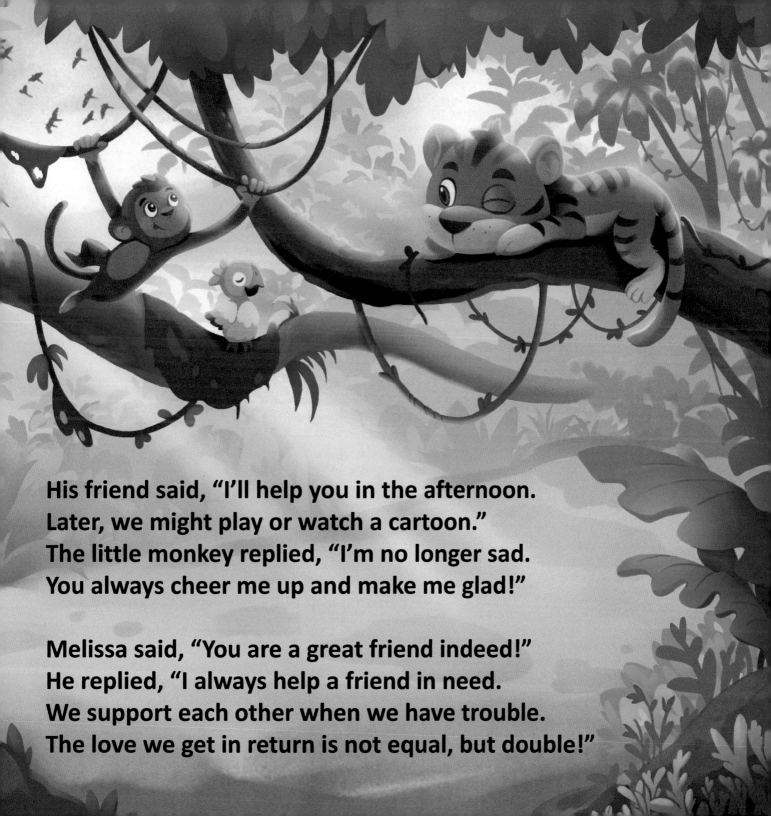

His friend said, "I'll help you in the afternoon.
Later, we might play or watch a cartoon."
The little monkey replied, "I'm no longer sad.
You always cheer me up and make me glad!"

Melissa said, "You are a great friend indeed!"
He replied, "I always help a friend in need.
We support each other when we have trouble.
The love we get in return is not equal, but double!"

Then, the giraffe took Melissa for a walk. She saw a lion and started the talk.

They both loved to draw,

and to ride a bike too!

The giraffe said, "Melissa, I'm so proud of you!"

"Now, you know a few ways to make friends,
but that is not where your mission ends.
Offer help and support if friends are upset.
True friendship is the best gift you can get!"

Melissa saw many different animals around.
They were playing together on the ground.
With glasses, or long necks, chubby and short,
the animals didn't mind each other's sort.

The lion started a story by looking up high.
"Friends make us shine like the stars in the sky.
For each act of friendship, true and sincere,
high in the sky, a new star will appear."

"Your star will shine brightly up in the sky
to remind others you're a friend on which to rely.
The more stars you get, the brighter the sky shines.
Together, they will form a beautiful stellar sign."

"I'll get my stars!" said Melissa. "They will be so bright!
My friendship stars will light up the sky every night!"
After Melissa had some more fun and play,
it was time to wake up and start a new day.

Melissa ran to the park and called out her name,
then asked other children to join in the game.
She enjoyed playing, she had lots of fun.
Melissa made many friends, not only one.

Be kind and say "sorry" when you are wrong.
That way, your friendships will last very long.
Friendship is built star by star, day by day.
So, ask yourself, "Has my star shone today?"

LET YOUR FRIENDSHIP STARS SHINE!

(color each star by doing an act of friendship)

Encourage your friends when they are sad

Make your friend feel good by giving a compliment

Offer a help when friends are in trouble

Show interest when your friend is speaking

Say sorry when you were wrong

Invite to play a game

Share your toys or snacks

Celebrate your friend's achievement

Show empathy to your friends

Forgive your friend

Go here to get your bonus coloring page

Dear little reader!

I'm sure that everyone once asked themselves the question what true friendship means. Hey, will you be my friend? Let's have fun and play together! But, what else does it mean to be a friend to someone? Can you be a good friend? Well, I didn't know the answers to those questions too when I was a kid! So, now I have written this book to show you the ways of making friends with no effort and to point out where the effort is needed to be a good friend.

Adorable animal characters have shown you the ways of keeping your friendship nice and warm-hearted! So, don't waste time, try the means this book suggests and let your Friendship Stars shine! I would be so happy to hear what you think about this book. It will help me a lot while I write the next one. Yes, there will be another book! There will be many more books to watch for and read in this series!

Can you guess where Melissa's dream might take her next time? How would she feel? If you tell me your idea, who knows, you might read about it in one of the next books. Wouldn't that be awesome?! I'm so excited to hear from you! You can write to me at elizabethcole.author@gmail.com or visit www.ecole-author.com.

Your input means a lot to me!
You can leave your review of this book here:

With love,
Elizabeth Cole

Made in the USA
Las Vegas, NV
11 October 2022